Ways to Save Your Marriage:

The Solution to Divorce and to Breaking Up

By

Joseph Correa

COPYRIGHT

© 2016 Finibi Inc

All rights reserved

Reproduction or translation of any part of this work beyond that permitted by section 107 or 108 of the 1976 United States Copyright Act without the permission of the copyright owner is unlawful.

This publication is designed to provide accurate and authoritative information in regard to the subject matter covered. It is sold with the understanding that neither the author nor the publisher is engaged in rendering marital advice. If marital assistance is needed, consult with a marriage specialist in the field that may address detailed issues. Marriage counsellors, psychologists and psychiatrists are all forms of assistance. This book is considered a guide and should not be used in any way otherwise.

ACKNOWLEDGEMENTS

This book is dedicated to my wife. Thank you for giving me the inspiration to make this book possible.

Ways to Save Your Marriage:

The Solution to Divorce and to Breaking Up

By

Joseph Correa

TABLE OF CONTENTS

Copyright

Acknowledgments

Introduction

Chapter 1: Marriage Counselling Done Right

Counselling: can it save your marriage?

Understanding your partner's emotional needs

Working together to save your marriage

Chapter 2: Valuing Communication

Constructive communication

Conflict resolution strategies

Positive talk and actions

Forgive and be forgiven

Chapter 3: Overcoming Marriage Problems

Recovery from an affair

Dealing with financial stress

Analyse your anger

Creating harmony in your relationship

Your relationship and your responsibilities: finding balance

Making second chances work: recovering from past relationships

Eliminating outside interference

Chapter 4: Reconnecting With Your Partner

Reduce tension

Rebuilding mutual respect

The importance of having fun

Share goals and your vision for the future

Rediscovering intimacy

Building lasting love

Chapter 5: Additional Thoughts on Marriage

Marriage is a work in progress

INTRODUCTION:

Marital problems are part of life and solutions to those problems are always available if you put in the time and effort. Figuring out what is missing or what needs to be fixed in the relationship is key so you can find the right tools to resolve the situation.

This book will help you confront common marital problems and will help you find multiple solutions to get you where you want to be.

Some of this book's content includes:

Chapter 1: Marriage Counselling Done Right

Counselling: can it save your marriage?

Understanding your partner's emotional needs

Working together to save your marriage

Chapter 2: Valuing Communication

Constructive communication

Conflict resolution strategies

Positive talk and actions

Forgive and be forgiven

Chapter 3: Overcoming Marriage Problems

Recovery from an affair

Dealing with financial stress

Analyse your anger

Creating harmony in your relationship

Your relationship and your responsibilities: finding balance

Making second chances work: recovering from past relationships

Eliminating outside interference

CHAPTER 1:

Marriage Counselling Done Right

Counselling: can it save your marriage?

When we are suffering from physical ailments, we know that we need to consult a doctor. But what if your relationship with your spouse is ailing? Can couples counselling really help to save your marriage?

According to researchers, marriage counselling has a 70-80% success rate. Experts say that counselling helps us to view our relationships more objectively, recognising how we contribute to the marital problems we are experiencing. Consider what would happen if each partner instead of trying to "fix" the other, focussed on reducing their own marriage-destroying habits and tendencies?

Getting an objective perspective on the deeply subjective issue of marital problems or marital breakdown can shed new light on old issues and point the way towards a successful resolution of marital problems and issues.

When should couples consult a counsellor?

Researchers have found that the primary problems experienced by couples are loss of connection and high levels of conflict. Counsellors agree that the sooner problems are attended to, the better. On average, most couples will have experienced problems for 6 years before considering counselling as an option. A quicker response time would reduce the amount of behavioural habituation that needs to be overcome.

How does it work?

The goal of counselling is not to present ready-made solutions, but to equip the couple with the tools they need to overcome their problems. The therapist interviews the couple together and sometimes requests individual interviews, then gives feedback. During a counselling program, couples should begin to notice minor but significant positive changes on a day to day basis. The basis of this success is mutual learning about and accommodation of each other's perspectives.

Professional counsellors won't take sides, will respect both partners and will strive for a calm atmosphere in which each participant has an opportunity to speak and air their views.

Sometimes one of the marriage partners is unwilling to undergo couples counselling, but the remaining partner can still benefit from relationship counselling and in time, persuade their spouse to join their effort to resolve mutual marital issues through couples counselling.

The aims of couples counselling:

- To determine the impact of external factors on the relationship.
- To determine what past factors impact on the present relationship.
- To improve communication.
- To gain an understanding of why arguments escalate.
- To negotiate and resolve conflicts.

Provided that couples counselling is embarked on with the mutual intention of resolving relationship issues and strengthening a relationship, it can be very helpful in restoring marriages. The counselling environment offers a neutral atmosphere for reflection and discussion that allows couples to be more objective about the issues they confront and facilitates problem-solving. This atmosphere is transferred to the home environment through tasks or assignments suggested by the counsellor.

Only you and your partner can save your marriage: but a good counsellor can help

There is no 'magic bullet' that can save a marriage, but professional counselling can certainly help couples to understand each other better and rebuild their relationships. If you choose this option, ensure that you consult an experienced couple's counsellor and be ready to make a personal effort to improve your marital relationship.

Understanding your partner's emotional needs

Staying together in marriage is a mutual effort, and that effort should be aimed at meeting the emotional needs of your partner. If each partner strives to fulfil the other's emotional needs, the result is a strong, happy marriage in which both spouses feel safe, comfortable and loved. This takes mutual understanding and a conscious effort on the part of both partners, but it is an investment in happiness and thus well worth undertaking.

Consider the following needs:

1. The need for affection

Although this is by no means the only emotional need in a marriage, it is one of the primary requirements for a happy relationship. Both men and women need to feel loved by their spouses. Hugs, kisses and kind words go a long way towards creating a lasting and satisfying relationship.

2. The need for sexual fulfilment

In marriage, each partner promises complete sexual fidelity, however one partner may have a greater need for sex than the other, and if this is not met within the marriage it will result in frustration, conflict and an increased chance of infidelity. Discuss your sexual needs openly with each other and determine how each partner can contribute to increased sexual fulfilment within the relationship.

3. Conversation

Meaningful conversation is essential to a strong relationship. Discussions on household requirements or other practical matters are not meaningful in this context. Make time to discuss your thoughts, feelings and experiences with your partner and be ready to listen as well as talk.

4. Fun

Keeping an element of fun and enjoyment in a relationship is important. Ensure that time is spent on mutually enjoyable activities on a regular basis. Share interests, hobbies and activities with one another.

5. Honesty

A marriage must be built on trust, and in order to be trusted, each partner needs to show their trustworthiness. Be truthful and open with one another and do not indulge in 'secret' activities. If you do not feel comfortable about disclosing an activity to your partner, you should probably not be indulging in it.

6. Domestic support

Helping each other round the house and with responsibilities such as child-rearing fulfils an important emotional need. Agree on ways I which each partner can contribute and be ready to go the extra mile.

7. Financial support

Although this may sound like a practical need rather than an emotional one, it can have severe emotional implications on a relationship when it is not present. Couples need to negotiate their financial contribution to the household as well as their contribution to domestic chores.

8. Family commitment

Marriage is the basis of the family unit. Each spouse must be committed to achieving wellbeing within the family unit and the extended family.

9. Respect

We all like to feel respected and even admired. When respect and admiration comes from those closest to us, we experience affirmation and feel appreciated. Without mutual respect, any marriage is doomed to failure or at least, unhappiness.

CHAPTER 2:

Value Communication

Save your marriage with constructive communication

The intimacy of marriage makes us well-acquainted with both the negative and positive traits of our partners. We know what issues they are sensitized to and our own social guardedness, the constraints of 'good manners', might no longer seem applicable. In many cases, this results in toxic communication that becomes a habit, destroying relationships.

When 'jokes' turn sour

For many couples, what started out as a bit of 'teasing' soon turns into a running battle – a sniping match. Sometimes well-targeted comments are used to denigrate your partner. What starts off as a bit of good natured teasing becomes a power game with each partner trying to gain the upper hand. Genuinely hurtful comments are presented as 'jokes' at the partner's expense. This can result in a tit-for-tat situation and alienation from a partner who has become an opponent or competitor rather than an ally.

Attack mode

Tackling a genuine issue is a sensitive business. All too often, this is done in 'attack mode' – a result of ongoing frustration that bursts forth in a devastating attack that targets the person rather than the problem. This counter-productive method of raising problems causes the partner to raise their defences and strike back in an effort to defend their integrity. The argument escalates and no solution to the issue that triggered it is found. Instead, each partner leaves the argument feeling emotionally bruised and all the more determined to defend their standpoint.

Revisiting the past

No relationship is without some history of past error. This may lead us to using our partners' previous errors or oversights as a weapon that gives us the moral high ground – or so we believe. We may say "You always…." or "You never…" citing examples. This kind of communication is sure to cause the recipient to raise defensive barriers. And that means that no solution will be reached.

Communication without aggression

No relationship without its issues or problems that need to be discussed, but this should be done calmly and without violating the integrity of the partner. In order to remain close as a couple, a competitive attitude needs to be eliminated. Verbal aggression, insults or accusations do not form part of a productive discussion. Instead of solving problems and bringing couples closer together, they cause animosity and drive the couple further apart. Words should be used as tools, not as weapons.

Tips for productive communication in marriage

- Don't be competitive and don't put each other down.
- Talk about how you feel about an issue and avoid blame.
- Listen carefully to your partner's perspective and try to understand it. Don't interrupt them.
- If you're not sure what they mean, ask questions.
- Be kind. Don't look for weak points or sensitivities to exploit.
- Acknowledge your partner's feelings as well as your own.
- Remember that you're in this together. You are each other's allies. Your partner is not your 'enemy'.
- Be ready to compromise. You don't have to 'win'.
- Listen to your tone of voice. An aggressive tone will put your partner on the defensive.

- Don't speak in anger. You will say something you wish you hadn't said. Call timeout if it's getting too much for you.

In order to keep communication open and effective, it is essential that your partner should not feel as if they are under attack, that you are judging them or treating them with contempt. Once communication becomes a perceived violation, it breaks down rather than builds relationships.

Conflict resolution strategies: Fair play in marital arguments

No marriage is without its conflicts, but conflict, when handled unfairly, can turn the home into a battleground and sour relationships. Communication experts and psychologists agree that unless certain ground-rules are observed, conflict can destroy relationships.

Consider the reason for the conflict

Conflicts should only be engaged in if solutions are being sought. In some cases, the conflict is related to a need to gain power over the partner, exacting vengeance, 'getting even' or competitiveness. Such conflicts are unproductive and break down rather than build relationships. Couples in conflict-ridden relationships need to consider the real reasons for the conflicts they engage in, ideally, with the help of a counsellor.

When you need to argue, play fair

There is no doubt that couples may experience issues and disagreements that will result in potentially uncomfortable conversations. Keeping problems to oneself only exacerbates them. In a close relationship such as a marriage, being able to express one's thoughts and feelings is necessary to a healthy relationship – even when you know that your spouse would prefer not to hear what you have to say.

1. Address issues calmly

Although one may feel emotional about the issue under discussion, keeping your argument calm and rational is essential in order to prevent a breakdown in communication.

2. Never argue in public

Arguing in public or worse yet in the presence of children, family members or friends is sure to cause embarrassment for your spouse. Since the intention of an argument should be a desire to explore solutions to an issue together, starting by causing a 'scene' will prevent this from the outset.

3. Remain relevant

All too often, spouses use arguments as a platform to air every grievance or perceived slight from the past. You may be arguing, but there is a specific reason for your disagreement. Remain current and relevant in order to create an atmosphere that is conducive to finding a solution.

4. Avoid insults and accusations

In order to solve problems as a team, it is essential that both partners should not feel as if they are under personal attack. Insults and accusations build barriers to effective communication and the resolution of problems.

5. Have a solution or goal in mind

Many arguments between couples are completely pointless. In order to determine whether arguments have sufficient validity to make them worth pursuing, determine whether there is any meaningful outcome that could be achieved. Arguing for the sake of arguing only drives couples further apart.

6. Allow your partner to save face

Knowing when a partner is trying to make peace or apologise is important. Continuing an argument after having received an apology or concession can be tempting, but does not allow for closure.

7. Arguments should be temporary

In a strong marriage, arguments should be rare and should pass quickly. If an argument persists owing to unresolved issues, it would be wisest to consider making use of a mediator such as a marriage counsellor to resolve the issue so that it can be left behind.

Research: Positive talk and affirming actions can save marriages

There are many myths surrounding the dissolution of marriage and the causes for divorce. For example, many people believe that infidelity is a primary cause of relationship problems, but research shows that infidelity was only cited by 20-25% of marriage counsellors as the reason for marital collapse. According to studies, 80% of marital breakdowns are caused by deterioration of intimacy.

Conflict and loss of connection

Marriages can fail at any time, but most commonly fail after 5 – 7 years owing to conflict while 10-12 years is the most common danger period for loss of intimacy. Thus married couples need to implement strategies to deal with conflict as well as find ways to increase intimacy and re-enforce their personal connection with each other. In this article, we will examine positive talk as a means of reinforcing intimacy.

Positive vs negative talk

No partner will ever be 'perfect' and the general stressors of daily life can cause partners to succumb more easily to irritation, criticising or showing contempt for their partners. Analysts believe that happy couples will have five positive interactions for every negative interaction, but after a number of years together, many marriage partners fail to acknowledge the positive characteristics they observe in their partners. Once an atmosphere of hostility or alienation exists, it may become more difficult for marriage partners to recognise the positive traits that initially attracted them to their spouses.

Researchers suggest that the key is the recognition of both positive and negative qualities while holding the partner in high esteem and providing affirmation of the partner's worth. They distinguish between 'Compassionate Love' in which this balance is achieved and unrealistic 'Romantic Love' in which the partner is glorified as 'perfect' and faults or weaknesses are not recognized.

Recognising the positives

Couples who want to overcome relationship issues should take time to reflect on their relationship. For this exercise, counsellors suggest that spouses create of a list of positives and negatives, at all times trying to ensure that the list of positives is longer and more thoughtfully complied than the list of negatives. Affective affirmation is essential to a happy marital relationship. In simpler terms, this implies finding ways of showing your partner that they are special, that you value them and don't take them for granted

Affirmation can be provided through words or actions. Affirming statements will acknowledge the positive qualities you see in your partner and the positive emotions that you associate with them. Affirming actions could be as simple as making morning coffee and serving it with a smile, exchanging small gifts or simply giving your partner a hug. Some psychologists believe that men may need affirmation even more than women do since women generally maintain closer family relationships and friendships.

Being consistent

It may be tempting to heap affirmation on a marriage partner and then taper off the positive interactions. Maintaining a consistent flow of positive interactions and affirmation is essential to a happy relationship. By focussing on positives, partners can strive for the ideal ratio of 1:20 or more negative to positive interactions. Negative interactions will still occur from time to time, but in general, both marriage partners will feel that they are dealing with an ally who loves them rather than an opponent who holds them in contempt.

Forgive and be forgiven

Love and marriage are riddled with pitfalls. Being human, we simply cannot be perfect. At some time or another, your spouse may do something that really hurts you. By the same token, you might hurt your spouse on certain occasions.

Holding onto grudges, anger and hurt destroys relationships. Marital arguments can turn into long litanies of the real and perceived slights of the past. Resentments easily surface as 'weapons' and the things that hurt you become tools with which you hurt your spouse. Being able to forgive each other is important to your happiness and ability to work together as couple, but forgiveness doesn't just happen. You have to go through a conscious process of forgiveness.

Talk about it

It's vital that we discuss the things that hurt us. Your partner may even be unaware of the hurtful behaviour. Launching into discussion in the heat of the moment can provoke a hostile or defensive reaction. Agree on a time to discuss what happened in advance. This gives you time to 'cool off' and prepares your partner for a serious discussion.

Use 'I' not 'You'

Ultimately, your hurt is about your feelings about a behaviour rather than the behaviour itself. Your partner may not even understand why you are so hurt by what they did, said or forgot to do and say. However, your feelings are what matters, and by understanding how you feel, your partner will more readily understand what triggered the hurt and be better able to avoid repeating the behaviour in the future. Telling someone what a bad person they are isn't going to bring you closer together, but expressing your feelings promotes understanding.

Forget about forgetting

Forgiveness does not bring on amnesia, but if you forgive or are forgiven, the situation has to be left behind. Forgiveness isn't about forgetting, it's about letting go. That means you can't raise the issue again. When discussing a situation that hurt you, avoid raking up past hurts or related incidents from the past and focus on the issue at hand.

Let go of anger

You have a right to anger as you have a right to any other emotion, but cherishing anger destroys relationships.

When you truly forgive, you are letting go of anger, bitterness and resentment. This isn't only good for your relationship, it's good for you and your mental and physical health.

Keep your perspective

Remember your priorities. In giving or receiving feedback about hurtful situations, your main priority should be preserving the connection between yourself and your spouse. The aim of discussing hurtful situations is to help your spouse get to know you better. It's not about 'winning', it's about achieving a greater understanding of each other so that you can become closer as couple.

When you are the one who needs to be forgiven

You may not understand or even want to believe that you have hurt your partner in some way, but it is essential that you should determine what caused them to feel hurt or wronged. This will help you to ascertain what you need to do differently in the future and what situations you should look out for. Even if you didn't mean to hurt your partner, you have to recognize and accept that you did. Apologise sincerely and suggest ways that you could have approached the situation in question more constructively in order to determine how you should behave in similar circumstances in future.

CHAPTER 3:

Overcoming marriage problems

Recovery from an affair: how to save your marriage

Affairs are not necessarily the end of a marriage, but there is no doubt that they place tremendous stress on the marriage relationship. The first steps in ending an affair should include a confession to the spouse and an honest undertaking to break all contact with the extra-marital interest. However, just taking these two steps does not necessarily ensure that the relationship will recover.

In many cases, those who indulge an affair may be unremorseful. They may feel that their spouse was lacking in some way and see this as justification for the affair. In such cases, both partners do not own responsibility for the breakdown in their relationship and neither feels it incumbent on them to take steps to restore the relationship.

Focus on your spouse's needs

Regardless of which partner was guilty of conducting an affair, the relationship is in need of help. Ultimately, we combat negatives by introducing positives. Assuming that both spouses would like to save their marriage, a mutual focus on their partner's needs and fulfilment is the only way to rebuild their relationship.

Although it easy to take a black-and-white view that the unfaithful partner is responsible for the threat to the relationship, both spouses need to recognize their contributions to the infidelity. For example, an unfaithful partner may cite a lack of attention to emotional and physical needs on the part of their spouse as the cause of an affair, and this must be recognized as a genuine fault and be addressed. The first step in rebuilding a marriage after infidelity is mutual apology and recognition of both the fault (infidelity) and the contributing motivations resulting from the 'innocent party's' handling of the relationship.

Eliminate anger, disrespect and demands

No relationship can be restored while these three elements exist. Couples who wish to restore their marriages after infidelity will first have to deal with their anger, learn to respect their partner again and focus on giving rather than taking. Both partners will have to consciously commit to protecting each other from hurt by considering their spouse's feelings in the process of rebuilding the marriage.

Understand and respect your spouse's perspective

This can be an extremely difficult process, but in order to rebuild a unified relationship, it is absolutely essential. A superficial reconciliation could take place, but if the cause of infidelity is not addressed in the relationship, there is a possibility of a recurrence.

Create a list of possible solutions

Although the actual affair may seem like the primary issue, it would not have taken place if the marriage had been perfectly healthy in the first place. Record all possible solutions and do not dismiss them out of hand.

Decide what should be done

Together, the couple should consider the possible solutions and which ones they feel the most positive about. A joint decision on which strategies to adopt should be made. If no solutions that generate mutual enthusiasm are found, more thought should be given to the issue.

Spend time together and keep working on your relationship

Rebuilding a relationship takes more than just good intentions. Partners in this situation will need to expend effort on meeting their spouse's emotional needs, rebuilding love and trust and strengthening their mutual bond.

Dealing with financial stress in marriage

When couples firs take the plunge and march down the aisle, money matters seem like the last thing that will affect their relationship. They m ay have (and should) have given some thought to the practicalities, but they seldom see money matters as being something that could threaten their relationships. But financial problems and issues have and do end marriages. First we'll look at why this happens, and then we will examine some solutions.

What triggers the problem?

1. Materialism: valuing possessions or marriage over the relationship

A recent study at William Patterson University found that if both partners in a relationship were highly materialistic, their relationship suffered. If one partner is materialistic, it can place strain on the spouse who feels that he or she is being used as a source of finance and has no other value to the spouse. Having the 'best' of everything won't make you happy, but having a strong marriage will.

2. 'Foolish' spending or excessive frugality

This is often a perception brought about by differing values. She may resent his spending on tech toys. He may feel that her penchant for designer shoes is excessive. Either way, when the spending habits of a spouse are perceived by their partner as 'foolish' and financial trouble ensues, it often ends in divorce. In fact, a study showed that 45% of couples in which one partner felt that their spouse's spending habits were excessive and unnecessary, ended in divorce. At the same time, excessive frugality can also cause problems. Berating one's spouse because they could have got the groceries for a few bucks less at a different store or should have shopped around more is an example of excessive frugality.

3. Who does the financial management in the home?

Most couples find that one partner is better than the other at managing family finances. It makes sense to allow this partner to manage the money that is used on joint expenses. At the same time, it's also important to communicate properly and consult each other about important financial decisions that may impact on home life. If this doesn't happen, marital strife ensues.

4. Not having a plan

Even when both partners are involved with family budgeting, a few incautious decisions can result in unpaid bills and financial stress. Some couples fail to budget, and only realise that they are in trouble when they find themselves unable to cover costs. At times of financial stress, accusations, bitterness and anger can all too easily rear their heads.

When financial issues impact on your marriage:

It's vital to remember that you both need to work together as a team to overcome this challenge. Fighting about it won't get you out of trouble.

- Remind yourselves that your marriage and your partner are more important to you than money or possessions. If this isn't strictly true for you, examine your value system critically.

- Wherever possible avoid debt and spending on credit. If you decide to go into debt, consult your partner, even if you will be solely responsible for the repayments. If debt is already impacting your marriage, consult a financial advisor to see if you can compound with creditors, consolidate your debt or defer payments. Discuss how you, as a couple, can avoid this situation in the future without placing blame on your partner.

- Make financial decisions together and know in advance what your plan for items like mortgage repayments, etc. will be. Budget carefully. If possible, keep a small 'emergency fund' for tough times.

- Share your family financial responsibilities. One partner may earn more and contribute more in real terms than the other, but both should contribute equally in terms of the degree of effort and proportionate financial contribution to the household.

- Find ways of saving money together and discuss the ground rules for individual spending including spending on luxuries.

Analyse your Anger

Anger is common in married relationships

As the pressures of work, finances and raising children mount, couples may find that they progress from being madly in love to just being mad. Working through issues takes an investment in time and a considerable amount of emotional energy. As a result, overburdened couples often leave their issues to fester, living with constant anger and resentment that bursts forth in the form of fights and unproductive arguments.

An angry outburst may relieve your feelings temporarily, but it's ultimately counter-productive. Anger can be a very frightening thing for the person on the receiving end, and since the trigger for pent up anger may be trivial, the spouse feels shocked and alienated. They tiptoe round their partner, becoming overly cautious and reserved or even avoid them as much as possible. The couple begins to grow apart, their sex-life suffers and the end result could be divorce – unless positive action is taken.

Anger and resentment are also bad for children. Parents become irritable and the home atmosphere becomes poisoned with resentful undercurrents, running battles, contemptuous glances and snide comments. Overcoming your anger has to be achieved as a couple, and everyone in the family will benefit.

Analysing and dealing with anger

The first step in overcoming anger: Make a conscious decision to deal with it and its real causes. If you are treasuring your anger as if it were some prized possession, you will never be able to deal with it constructively with your partner. Get counselling if you find the idea of letting go of and resolving anger and resentments difficult.

Find your trigger points: What makes you irritable? It may not even be something your spouse can't help with. Sometimes we take out our frustrations on others even when they don't contribute. For example, a stressful commute in rush hour traffic can make one irritable enough to become genuinely angry about trivial issues that otherwise would not be worth mentioning. Think about how you can reduce or avoid these stressful situations. In the example above, our commuter could consider taking public transport or leaving a little earlier or later so that they can miss the traffic.

Now consider your spouse's behaviours. What makes you angry? How do you contribute to that behaviour? For example, if you're an extremely decisive person, your partner may defer to you and you may get angry at them for not participating in decisions. In this example, the bad dynamic is contributed to by both partners.

Revisit the introduction to this e-book and study the portion on emotional needs. Do you feel that your spouse is neglecting your emotional needs? Which ones? In marriage, practical needs like financial and domestic support also become emotional needs. Again, consider your situation objectively. The outwards symptom (neglect of an emotional need) may result from or be aggravated by something that you habitually do.

Talk about it

But remember not do so when you are actually feeling angry. You will sound unreasonable, you may say things that you don't actually mean, or state them in a manner that is designed to hurt. Wait until you can discuss your issues calmly, respectfully and courteously – and let your spouse know that the discussion is going to happen and when it will take place. With your spouse, look for practical solutions to the real issues that have been causing anger and resentment between you. It may help to remind yourselves about each other's good qualities before you begin! If you and your spouse struggle to resolve issues, consider visiting a counsellor who can act as an impartial mediator.

Implement the solutions

Remember that your solutions will take an effort for both partners. The 'angry' spouse has to minimize their contribution to the 'annoying' behaviour and the partner needs to make an honest effort. If this is done, resist the urge to criticise their effort if it wasn't done in quite the way you would have done it. Acknowledge that they are trying and thank them sincerely. If you have to remind your spouse about what was agreed, resist the urge to do so with aggression. Be polite and show respect.

Make time together

Spending time together keeps couples close and better able to deal with problems when they arise. Read the chapter on the importance of fun in marriage to see just how having fun together helps to make your marriage stronger and commit to a weekly 'date'.

Creating harmony in your relationship

People in committed relationships apply various ways of interacting. Some seem to constantly be debating and arguing, other appear withdrawn and distant from another whilst maintaining cordiality, and yet a few seem able to remain warm and loving towards each other throughout many years of marriage. Is it possible to become like them?

You have probably observed other couples who seem to be in continuous conflict. They fight, they argue and they shame each other. According to research, those of us who are raised in households where this kind of interaction is the norm are more likely to carry it over into our own married lives. If your relationship is riddled with conflicts, do you really want your children to believe that this is what marriage should be like? Wouldn't you like to change the situation for your own good, for the sake of your children and the good of your marriage?

Having the occasional spat is not necessarily bad for your marriage, but if it becomes habitual, it results in defensiveness, withdrawal and stubbornness. The problem with all three of these is that they do not contribute to the resolution of issues.

What is your primary focus in your marriage?

All these sources of disharmony can be traced back to self-interest. Marriage counsellors agree that putting your partner's feelings first, is the key to marital harmony. Obviously, your own needs are still important. No-one should become a martyr, but taking your partner's needs, desires and wellbeing as a priority can make you both happier – especially if you both commit to doing this. However, the magic of being considerate is that it promotes reciprocal consideration in the spouse or partner. Love and be loved. Be considerate and get consideration.

Create harmony as a team

When we focus on our own desires and wishes as a primary consideration, we are excluding ourselves form the team of two that makes up a marriage. The result is disharmony. On the other hand, mutual consideration builds your 'team'. Because you support each other, harmony is fostered. Note that this is a two-way street. Explore, respect and strive to fulfil your partner's needs. Then do the same thing in order to determine what you most need and require from your partner. In this way, you can enter a transitional phase of compromise and negotiation that will result in a harmonious, supportive and happy relationship in which each partner gives and each partner receives according to their needs.

- Consciously reject the belief that continuous or regular disharmony is a natural condition for married couples.
- Understand that heated arguments and continual disharmony will result in emotional distance.
- Resolve to demonstrate mutual consideration, explore each other's needs, give kindness and receive kindness.

If your relationship has been characterized by conflict and emotional estrangement in the past, you will first need to deal with your issues and reconnect. Read the chapter on reconnecting with your loved one as well as the chapter on communication to find helpful advice on doing this.

Your relationship and your responsibilities: finding balance

The modern life is a busy one. In most marriages, both partners work – and these days – the border between workplace and home life has become blurred. People in demanding careers often ending up working from home till late at night, reading their emails when they wake up in the morning or at the family dinner table or doing some or other work-related task from home.

Back on the home front, there are children to be cared for, chores to be done and meals to be prepared. With such a hectic schedule, can we wonder at the fact that so many couples seem to 'grow apart' or end up 'living past' each other? How can we balance our careers, our family responsibilities and our personal relationships with our marriage partners?

What are your priorities?

Let's face facts: whatever we consider the most important is what we attend to most. The things we consider 'less important' suffer. But do we really have to be supermen and superwomen? We don't have to be brilliant at absolutely everything, and we can be great at what we prioritize. Be honest with yourself: what's more important to you, your marriage, home chores or your career? All too many of us will say it's our careers that matter most.

But is that really true? Wouldn't a happy family life and a loving relationship with your spouse bring you much more satisfaction and happiness than a pat on the back from the boss? You can still do fine at work, but you will have to manage your time carefully.

At work:

- Plan your time carefully so that you are able to attend to your most important tasks. If you're in a position where you can delegate less important tasks, do so.

- Learn to say 'no'. You've heard this a thousand times, but do you do it? If you are asked to do something when your schedule is already full, you can tactfully ask your employer to move some deadlines around or indicate priorities so that your work can fit into the working day.

- If your home life has been suffering as a result of constant work, even when you are theoretically off-duty, be honest with your employer about the situation, and ask them to understand that you have been working beyond your capacity and must attend to your home-life more diligently.

- If you are self-employed, this gets a bit harder. Look at outsourcing simple tasks to a part-timer, piece worker, freelancer or sub-contractor. You will find that you have more time to work on profitable tasks within a normal workday, and you may even boost your business earnings.

At home

- Make non-negotiable time for attending to household duties and your children's needs, and make that all-important time for being alone with your marriage partner. Discuss your proposed schedule with your spouse and ask for their input. Planning and scheduling time with your spouse and family may sound cold-blooded, but if you don't do it, you may find that it doesn't happen at all.
- Don't bring work to the dinner table. Have a proper family meal seated at table with the TV off. Mealtimes are a wonderful opportunity to become closer as a family. Cell phones, laptops and other distractions do not belong at the dinner table.

- Discuss the division of household chores with your marriage partner. If both of you are working hard on your careers, chores and parenting duties should be evenly and fairly divided. Not doing this can result in resentments and future arguments.

- If you foresee a period where you will have to put in extra hours in order to advance your career, discuss it with your husband or wife. Determine the impact it will have on your family life and family members, what adjustments would need to be made to agreed responsibilities, and set a time limit for this disruption. Work is important, but your family and spouse are even more important.

- Agree on time off from the daily grind with your partner. You both need time to relax and share enjoyment away from your many responsibilities. (see the chapter on the importance of fun)

Making second chances work: recovering from past relationships

If you have been divorced before, are a widow or widower or marrying someone else after a previous serious relationship failed, you will have to think carefully about how you are going to make your second marriage or serious relationship work. Taking the baggage of the past into a new relationship can get you into serious relationship trouble that could end in divorce or emotional estrangement. Psychologists, marriage counsellors and those who have overcome the pitfalls of a second serious relationship agree that there are steps you can take to ensure you get it right this time around.

First and foremost: resolve that you will make your marriage work, no matter what it takes. Once you have made this commitment to yourself, you are ready for the next step:

Your old love is not part of your new relationship

Whether you were bereaved or divorced, there is one, very important thing you need to realize: You should never, ever compare your new spouse with your departed or ex-loved one. It simply isn't fair, and it could ruin your chances of a happy relationship.

Realise that it is a natural tendency to view your departed loved one (and sometimes even ex-lovers) through rose-tinted glasses and that your new partner has his or her own set of positive qualities that you love and respect them for. Let go of guilt for choosing a new partner. It is natural to seek a new mate when you have been left to live alone – but be sure that you have processed your grief properly and get help if this is not the case. This last point is valid for those who have been through a divorce too – there is always grief in the death of a relationship.

If you still harbour bitterness towards a previous partner, don't allow it to colour your present relationship. You are starting afresh and though you can't forget your past, you should not let it influence your attitude towards your second attempt at wedded bliss – unless that influence is the resolution to get it right this time!

What went wrong with your past relationship?

If you were in a relationship that failed, determining what went wrong is a difficult process, and you will be opening up some old wounds. A study found that spouses who had previously been divorced and whose second marriages were more lasting than their first marriages had a significant characteristic in common: **they accepted part of the blame for the breakdown of their previous relationship.**

It takes two to make a marriage, and in most cases, it takes two to make marriage problems too. It's important to discuss this with your partner. Keeping it secret will cause guilt and your partner may fear or be jealous of your previous relationship or relationships if you don't take this important step. By the same token, your partner should be willing to be open about past relationships and why they soured. Together, you can resolve to try a different approach this time around and build a stronger, lasting relationship.

Eliminating outside interference in your marriage

Friends, relatives, work and even children can all interfere with your marriage relationship. Sometimes outside activities are partly to blame. How can you eliminate destructive interference from outside your relationship?

Work and outside activities

If your spouse seems to prefer spending time at work or visiting his or her friends to spending time with you, you have to ask yourself why this is happening. In some cases, an unhappy spouse will avoid the home environment as much as possible because they are not feeling fulfilled by their home life. It's easy to blame your partner for neglecting you, but there is probably some way in which you contribute to the problem.

If, for example, there is a lot of conflict in your relationship, you need to confront the fact that your role in the conflict is making for an uncomfortable home-life and take appropriate steps to deal with it. Sometimes, there is a lack of shared interests. Can you find a way of addressing this by participating in or taking an interest in your spouse's favourite interests and activities? Of course, some people are just very career driven. Discuss the issue with your partner (refer to the chapter on balancing work and responsibilities for ideas).

Friends

You may have been accustomed to sharing all your personal information with your friends, but your marriage is an intimate relationship. That means that there are some things you simply shouldn't discuss with your friends. You cannot be a faithful and loving spouse if you are criticising your partner behind his or her back. Sometimes, we even exaggerate the problems in our marriages to get the sympathy of friends. This is a betrayal of your spouse's trust.

Create boundaries and do not cross them. If you are having problems in your marriage and would like advice, save your discussion for someone who can really help you to resolve issues and who is impartial, and will keep them confidential: a trained marriage counsellor. If your friends cross the line and begin to criticise your spouse to you, stop them in their tracks. Your marriage is between you and your spouse. Show your friends that you will not tolerate interference.

Children

Your children need lots of love and attention and you should not deny them that, but they should not be used as an excuse to avoid or neglect time alone with your partner. If you are doing this, or your marriage partner appears to be using parental responsibilities to avoid you, you need to identify the real issues in your relationship and deal with them. Children also needs rules. Disciplines such as bed-times and times when they should not disturb you unless it is an emergency can be laid down for older children who are able to understand them.

Parents and in-laws

Your own parents are used to sharing in your life and advising you, but once you are married, they do not form part of the relationship. Do not allow your parents to criticise your spouse and don't criticise your spouse to your parents. Handle the issue in much the same way as you would prevent possible interference form friends.

One in ten marriages end because of interference from parents-in-law. While you can tell your own parents to allow you space to solve your own marital issues, it can be difficult when you are dealing with your spouse's parents. This issue is best dealt with by discussing the issue calmly with your spouse and enlisting their assistance in limiting the interference. We all know the maxim that no one is ever good enough for the sons or daughters of doting parents!

CHAPTER 4:

Reconnecting with your partner

Reducing tension and conflict in relationships

All married couples experience times when there are tensions, anger, conflict or unresolved issues in their relationships. Learning how to reduce these tensions and move forward with the relationship is essential to marital bliss. Many established couples find that in time, they automatically perform certain tension-reducing actions and behaviours.

Expose tensions, deal with them and leave them behind

Identifying the source of marital tensions is essential. Avoidance tactics only serve to aggravate and escalate tensions. By working together, couples can reduce marital tension by being frank about the issues that are causing tension in the relationship, find mutually acceptable strategies to deal with them, and ultimately resolve them. However, this process can be complex and guidance may be needed.

'Sleeping on it'

Sometimes, a good night's rest brings a new perspective. What may have seemed vitally important at the time when it occurred becomes trivial when re-considered calmly. Many therapists recommend that couples agree to continue discussions or arguments on the following day and many couples find that this perspective helps them to resolve issues more effectively.

Take a short break

When arguments become overly heated and unproductive, taking a few minutes to become calmer and reconnect can save the day. Counsellors report that a break as short as 30 seconds allows couples to become calmer and regain perspective.

Recognising a fault

Marriage and family therapists recognize the importance of the apology and expressions of empathy. Although we don't always like admitting to our contribution to a problem, being honest and acknowledging our partners' feelings can break tension. When we notice ourselves being particularly defensive, we need to recognize that we are aware of our contribution to an issue and should acknowledge it openly.

Touch and affection

Love is the basis of marriage. When confronted with stressful issues, we often forget the importance of re-connecting through touch. Holding and comforting one another may not resolve practical issues, but it does remind couples of their mutual bond of affection and relieves tensions.

Quality time

Busy couples may find that the only time they really make contact is when important practical issues need to be resolved. Making time for one another and the relationship is essential to the maintenance and longevity of marriages. By cultivating and maintaining mutual understanding and creating an atmosphere in which each partner feels comfortable relaxing and just being themselves, overcoming periods of tension or conflict is made easier.

Remember priorities

In a marriage, there are three priorities: you, your spouse and your marriage. If tensions and arguments are not conducive to the wellbeing of any one of these three elements, they should not be given importance or be allowed to adversely impact the relationship.

Deal-breakers

Affairs, addictions and abuse cause severe tension in marriage. Almost any other issue can be resolved mutually, but if any of these three elements is present in a relationship, it becomes the duty of the partner who is guilty of these behaviours to eliminate them or face the risk of a permanent breakdown of the marriage. In any of these instances, professional help may be needed in order to reduce marital tensions, even after the elimination of the behaviour has taken place.

<u>Rebuilding mutual respect</u>

Mutual respect is the basis for a strong foundation that keeps your marriage relationship healthy, happy and fulfilling for both partners. This is not just an opinion or a common-sense statement, it has been proven in research. No matter what problems your marriage is undergoing, they will not be resolved if mutual respect is absent.

What is mutual respect?

In practical terms, 'mutual respect is shown in the following ways:

- By being considerate and courteous towards your marriage partner.
- By avoiding behaviours such as name-calling, insults, sarcasm and one-upmanship.

- By taking your partners values, needs and opinions into account.
- By consulting your partner in decision-making situations – especially if these will affect home life.
- By taking an active interest in your partner's activities and interests.
- By being ready to compromise when you and your partner have divergent views.
-

Respect is established through behaving respectfully. It is a 'do as you would be done by' situation. Respect is lost when your partner feels that you are not treating them with respect or when you break their trust in you.

Rebuilding mutual respect in your relationship

Unfortunately, treating each other with disrespect becomes a habit for some couples, and habits can be difficult to break. Sometimes, there is so much hurt and anger as a result of mutual disrespect that each partner refuses to change their behaviour unless the other partner does so first. Sometimes, one partner tries to change their behaviour and is rebuffed by the other partner. Some things to remember while working to rebuild mutual respect:

- You cannot change your partner's behaviour, you can only work on improving your own.

- Avoid the pitfall of using an effort to rebuild respect as an excuse to criticize your partner's behaviour.

The first step in rebuilding mutual respect can be very difficult. It means focussing on your treatment of your partner rather than their treatment of you. Revisit the examples of mutual respect above. If you treat your partner in this way, the chances of their reciprocating are excellent – but it may take time when wounds run deep. Once mutual respect has been re-established, it becomes easier to deal with other problems such as the way in which couples tackle problems, differences of opinion and cope with personal differences.

Learning to accept and appreciate personal differences

'Opposites attract' is often a truism. Ironically, once couples are in a long-term relationship, they may expend a lot of energy on trying to 'change' their partner to be more like them or to fit an image of the 'ideal' partner that they have formed in their minds. Accepting and respecting your personal differences is important to the success of your marriage. Your partner may differ in personality, values or aspirations. Tolerance, acceptance and even appreciation of the ways in which you and your partner differ is very important in maintaining respect in marriage. These differences can make you stronger as a couple – if you allow them to.

The importance of fun in marriage – recapturing the magic

The majority of marital breakdowns are the result of a loss of intimacy. Couples may say that they have 'drifted apart' owing to the demands of daily life and the responsibilities of a home and family. When couples are courting, they spend time having fun together, but once married, they see each other on a daily basis and may overlook the need to spend quality time in each other's company.

Having fun builds relationships

Just spending time together isn't enough to keep couples close. Research has shown that couples who make a point of doing unusual or exciting things together are far more likely to rate their marriage as 'happy' and are thus much less likely to divorce.

'Date night' helps to keep couples together

Every couple experiences pressure from the demands of daily life, and this can all too often lead to conflict and stress. By setting aside time to enjoy a 'date' away from the pressures and concerns of family life, couples are able to spend time enjoying each other's company.

Couples can spend fun time together at home too, but invariably, children and household responsibilities intervene. Most experts suggest that couples should attempt to go out on a 'date' that's just for the two of them at least once a week.

Dates don't have to be expensive. Art-exhibitions, moonlight picnics or even taking a pleasant walk in the park together are all excellent opportunities for a date with your spouse. Agree to leave all conflicts and concerns behind during the special time you dedicate to sharing fun and pleasure. There will be plenty of opportunities to deal with serious issues at another time.

Having a little fun every day

Sharing laughter is a wonderful way of building intimacy. See the funny side of things and share laughter with your spouse. Did one of your children say something cute or funny today? Was there a funny story in the news? Share your laughter and become closer as a couple.

Play is for adults too. Join each other in a board game or tackle an online game together. Go tenpin bowling with your partner or attempt a round of mini-golf. Toss a Frisbee around the garden or go for a swim together. Don't let your relationship become all work and no play.

Share a leisure activity that you both enjoy or take classes together. Join an amateur dramatics club or take pottery classes – any opportunity for fun is an opportunity to build your relationship.

Be best friends

Researchers have found that happily married men often refer to their wives as their 'best friends'. A study found that men saw shared activities as being the root of their 'friendship' with their spouses. Women were more likely to see intimate conversation as the basis of a strong relationship. By combining the two – sharing activities and intimate conversation – couples can build a stronger relationship that is more likely to withstand the inevitable pressures and conflicts that arise in marriage.

Share goals and your vision for the future

When you first got married, you had a vision for your future, but as time goes on, your goals and vision may no longer be the same as they were back then. You may even have completely differing sets of goals, dreams and future plans. This could be a source of conflict at worst and at best will prevent you from being completely supportive of one another. Once again, it's time to sit down and talk.

Sharing your vision helps you reach your goals

In order for a marriage to succeed, team work is essential, but no couple can work effectively as a team if they're both striving towards differing goals. It's like having your own business. Each team member needs to know what goals they are working towards and what the strategy for the future is. Without this knowledge, efforts are uncoordinated and unproductive. But when goals and visions for the future are shared and each person knows what their contribution to the master-plan will be, wonderful things can happen. You achieve synergy, a state in which your combined efforts far exceed anything that would have been achieved through working in isolation.

Discuss your vision and goals and be ready to compromise

No marriage partner should expect their spouse to subscribe completely to their vision of the future. That would be the same as expecting them to live their life for you. The keyword to remember is 'sharing'. If you aren't both enthusiastic about future plans, striving to achieve them will be fraught with conflict.

That doesn't mean that you should necessarily give up on your vision for the future, but you may have to alter it slightly to accommodate your partners dreams and ambitions. Get together to brainstorm your way forward.

Capture all your ideas for the future together

Where would you like to be as a couple in five years' time? In ten years? By the time you retire? To begin with, just capture all the ideas. You may not be able to do everything on the list, but it's a good starting point for determining your future strategies and of gauging how both partners' input can be incorporated into your master-plan for the future. Once you have a full list, you can prioritize and categorize the elements you've captured. What is most important? Are some goals and plans related to each other?

Craft a vision that you both love

What do you and your partner see as an ideal lifestyle? Use your shared ideas to craft a vision statement that you both feel enthusiastic and excited about. Don't worry about how you will achieve it yet. That's the next step in the process.

What milestones will you have to reach to achieve your vision?

In any long journey, there are milestones along the way. These help you to keep track and determine if you are still on the right route and making good progress. Decide together what your journey towards your vision will need to consist of. For example, if you would like to achieve financial independence, you will want to begin by paying off your mortgage. When can you realistically expect this to happen? Can it be fast-tracked? What sacrifices would you and your partner have to make and are you willing to make them?

Set up and track your time-line

Revisit your mutual goals regularly and don't forget to celebrate achievements. You'll be amazed at how much you can achieve together when working towards a common goal.

Rediscovering intimacy

When you first got together as a couple, sex was absolutely wonderful, but then life happened. Your time got filled up with work commitments, kids and household chores. The intimacy began to taper off and bed became a place for sleeping only. Can you rekindle the magic? Experts say that you can – if you both commit to it.

Make a commitment to each other

Before you can hope for this to work, you need to clear away tensions, arguments and negative emotions. Recognise your love for each other and commit to rekindling the intimacy in your relationship.

Take ten minutes a day

Make a special time when you and your partner will discuss your progress together. You might find that you are a little nervous about this at first – but you are talking to your life-partner – so this topic is of importance to both of you. Discuss any obstacles to healthy sex. Are you both overtired? Do your kids give you enough privacy? Look for solutions to the obstacles that are keeping you apart.

Re-live some of your most magical moments with your partner. What did he or she do that you thought was absolutely amazing? Talking about sex in a non-sexual situation gives you and your partner an excellent opportunity to explore each other's needs and desires. You need to be able to do this without feeling embarrassment.

You can even share each other's fantasies. You may not want to live them out – we all have fantasies about things that we would never do – but you may find that discussing your sexual fantasies together gives you some fresh ideas and brings you closer together as a couple.

Rekindle romance

What were the special little things you used to do for each other that have fallen by the wayside? Perhaps you used to exchange small gifts or give each other a massage. By treating your marriage partner as a lover, you can rekindle romance and with it, reignite your sex life.

Take time out away from day to day responsibilities and commit to a regular date night when you just have fun together. And if you can, consider taking a second honeymoon while your folks, family members or reliable friends take care of your kids. Consider packing the kids off for a camp during school holidays and taking a romantic break away together during that time. A change of scene and a romantic setting could be just what you need to get things going.

Sharing activities helps

The more activities you can share, the more you will rekindle closeness and emotional connection – and these two foundation stones can help you to rebuild your relationship, bringing love, affection and sexual intimacy back into your marriage naturally.

Building lasting love in marriage

At some time in your life, you will have seen elderly couples who gaze at each other like star-struck lovers. Could you achieve such lasting love in your marriage? What is their secret?

Commitment to 'forever'

Just repeating vows doesn't make them 'real' for you. Decide with your spouse that divorce will never be an option. Together, you will overcome whatever life throws at you. Every conversation, every decision and your personal attitude to your relationship should be based on this principle. The two of you will stay together no matter what it takes. Be aware that relationships take work, and be committed enough to your marriage to be ready to make the effort. Just sitting back and waiting for you partner to 'make you happy' isn't going to get you anywhere. You will both have to work on your relationship and keep on working even when the going gets tough.

Your spouse is the most important person in your life

Putting your spouse first means giving of yourself. As the old cliché says, "There is no 'I' in' team'." If you both resolve to put each other first, neither of you will ever lack love, support and consideration. The exciting thing about taking this approach is that it keeps on growing – the more you give to your spouse, the more you will receive in return. If you find yourself doing something out of pride or selfishness (after all, we are only human) apologise sincerely and start over. Remember all the things you love about each other and maintain respect. Having 'faults' and 'weaknesses' is just part of being human. Stay focussed on the positives that brought you together in the first place. Every day is a new day in which you can learn more about each other and grow your relationship.

Be honest with each other

Sharing you lives together means that you have to share both the good and the bad times. It also means owning up when you did something wrong or when you feel that your partner has hurt you in some way. There should be no secrets between you. Don't allow resentments to fester. Talk about them constructively and rationally and remember that listening is as important as talking. There are always two sides to every story, and your partner's opinion should be as important to you as your own. You may not always agree with each other, but you don't have to allow that to spoil your relationship. If you find yourselves at an impasse, consider consulting a counsellor to guide you through your differences.

Spend quality time together

Your best times should be the times you share with your life partner. Work together to create special times, special memories and times that are for the two of you alone. Keep the magic alive in your relationship by getting away from the humdrum routine and simply enjoying each other's company. Remember: your marriage isn't about your job, paying the bills, planning meals and household chores for the week or even your children. Your relationship is about you and your partner. Make lots of opportunities for positive interactions and discover that love can grow and mature as the years go by.

CHAPTER 5:

Additional Thoughts on Marriage

Marriage is a work in progress. As we grow in life our perspectives change and so do our needs. This in turn changes who we are and what we need.

Growing together as a couple makes this process easier and a lot more fun. Creating common goals and reaching them will help you remain happily together over the years and will notice you will both be going in the same direction. Enjoy the journey and enjoy each other.

Life is too short to let someone special leave your side. Be persistent and don't give up on the one you care the most about.

www.ingramcontent.com/pod-product-compliance
Lightning Source LLC
Chambersburg PA
CBHW052123070526
44586CB00016B/2060